T0197181

The Remedy Within

Eleanor Hassall

BALBOA.
PRESS
A DIVISION OF HAY HOUSE

Balboa Press books may be ordered through booksellers or by contacting:

Balboa Press
A Division of Hay House
1663 Liberty Drive
Bloomington, IN 47403
www.balboapress.com
1 (877) 407-4847

Print information available on the last page.

ISBN: 978-1-5043-0102-2 (sc)
ISBN: 978-1-5043-0103-9 (e)

Balboa Press rev. date: 02/12/2016

I would like to dedicate this book to
my children and grandchildren.

Contents

INTRODUCTION

This book was written to reach people diagnosed with cancer with the hope that they might find different ways to help themselves. I was diagnosed with terminal lung cancer, which had spread to one of my adrenal glands, as well as a small tumour on the top of my bowel, which has been removed. I describe experiences that have helped me and I am keen to share these experiences with others. When you receive a diagnosis of cancer it is shocking news that you don't want to hear and you will think 'This cannot be happening to me' 'I have so much to do yet', and 'Am I dreaming?' It takes a while to come to terms with this and to pick yourself up and get ready to rescue yourself. My story outlines the holistic steps I have taken to nurture myself. I hope that they will help you get stronger in mind and body and spirit too.

I happen to be put in a chemo room the other day while I got bloods taken and I was so shocked at the people coming and going from all walks of life, my heart went out to them. We need a miracle.

I trust in spirit and this is my journey and I hope you will join me.

Through this emotional journey you can learn a lot about yourself and you will go deep within asking 'Why me?' The first step I took was to change my mind set, to believe, stop thinking negatively, block any bad thoughts and to see myself as well and radiant.

> *"Every human being is the author of his own health or disease."*

Buddha

We will go through this healing journey together are you ready ………….. let us get started.

CHAPTER 1

The Beginning

I have been guided by the angels to write this book to help others with their emotional journey through cancer and they kindly provided the title too. I thought at first "Me write a book you must be joking!" as I am not that great at expressing myself but I've done it and I hope it helps in someway and that you will benefit from reading it.

I am just an ordinary person who has led an extraordinary life. I was born in Belfast, Northern Ireland but spent my early years growing up in a little place called Ballynahinch, a lovely country village.

We had a very happy loving family and I remember the laughter and even though we hadn't much money we were blessed and content. My father Moses was the barber in the village and was a very humble caring man who had a great sense of humour, everyone loved him. Mum was very loving but didn't hold back when she had something to say! I remember her father had said she had such a tiny nose because she was behind the door when the noses were given out and I told her she wasn't there when the tongues were given out. We loved to laugh and sometimes I laughed so hard I cried. Mum loved her fashion and worked as a seamstress and she enjoyed a bit of craic (Irish for chatting). They both were very hard workers. I had two older brothers Roy and Derick and an older sister Gwen. We remain very close even though we now live so far apart. My mum described Gwen as "Cut out to be a lady but they lost the pattern". It wasn't the case with me. From a young age I was very different. I had migraines, nose bleeds and fainted all the time but in those days you just got on with it, which I did. I was always fascinated with my dreams and even then was so connected with my heart. I remember crying a lot at the Lassie programmes and maybe that is where I got my love for animals from as we always had a dog. Life was great but then we moved to the big city of Belfast and it was so built up compared to the country living. A few years later the sectarian troubles got really bad and I remember our streets being policed by armoured vehicles and standing at our front door listening to gunshots. I felt secure and safe with both police and army on our streets and as long as you stayed in your own area of religion you felt more secure. It was very sad when I think back on it but it was a normal way of life for us then. You were searched at anytime, anywhere and the thing that puzzled me was when there was a bomb scare people just stood outside the shop until they got the all clear. What if a bomb had gone off? There were bombs exploding all over Northern Ireland in restaurants, hotels, pubs and a lot of innocent lives were taken, you just hoped you weren't in the wrong place at the wrong time. Even the police had to check their cars for bombs before they went to work in the morning.

The highlight of my day was walking home from school with a macaroon bar which I bought with my bus money, simple things give me comfort. Our fridge was a wooden box outside in a small yard with wire mesh over the front of it and when the snow came and the milkman couldn't get through we had to buy some condensed milk to put in our tea. Guess who was very happy then.

I left school at 15 and worked as a shorthand typist, which was a popular profession open to the majority of girls then. I wasn't happy working in this area as it was all too rigid and serious for me and I therefore changed direction and moved to work with the mentally ill people. I worked there for 7 years and become a Mental Health Officer. I loved being employed in such a rewarding job. It helped open my eyes to how thin the line is between sanity and insanity. I appreciated my life more and looking back this is were my holistic work started.

I met my husband Keith when I was 18. He lived about 30 minutes drive from Belfast in a place called the Cottown. He had a strong English accent, short hair and was in the Merchant Navy and when he came into some of the areas of Belfast he was asked for identification as they thought he was a soldier. Consequently, when we went out for the night I did all the talking as soldiers and police were targeted at this time. I married at 25 and have been blessed with 4 wonderful children in my lifetime; Karl, Paul, Richard and Elle. I remember having a dream that when my first child was born he was an African with tight curly hair and it caused great laughter in the family but guess where we ended up?! Yes! South Africa! I have always been interested in analysing my dreams from a young age and this was going to benefit me through my life.

CHAPTER 2

Africa

We moved to South Africa, as Keith was made redundant as an engineer on the ferries. Leaving my family was very very difficult as we were so close and in those days we didn't have Skype and phone calls were expensive.

I didn't know what to expect when flying out with Keith and my first 2 children Karl and Paul, would it be a jungle and wild animals everywhere? South Africa was a beautiful country and the people so friendly it was a real adventure but at times I was left on my own as Keith travelled a good bit with his job. Thank goodness I had my boys. I loved the African people. They lived so simply as long as they had a tree to sit under and a loaf of bread to eat and they were always so happy. They made me wonder what happened to the simple way of life? We have all lost those roots and it is sad. I remember listening to the Africans sing as they worked, such wonderful voices and you felt such joy. We stayed in a hotel for a while and then moved into a flat for a few months in New Germany while we waited for our furniture to be shipped out. It wasn't enjoyable lying on blow up beds but we had a balcony and barbeque so we survived!

We moved into a beautiful house in Marionhill area near Pinetown by a nature reserve and had a great time there. The South African people are so hospitable and opened their doors to you, really nice people and we made and still have lots of great friends there. However, my eldest boy Karl was always sick as it was so humid and the doctor recommended that we would be better moving to Johannesburg.

We realised that close proximity to the nature reserve could be causing these illnesses after seeing large birds holding rats in their mouths and washing them in the swimming pool. We had 2 legavaans in the roof space and heard them crawling about at night and they probably swam in the pool. I remember the first time I saw them when I was gardening. I looked up at the side of the house and two really large legavaans (about 3 foot long) were sunning themselves on the wall. I just froze but after learning they were not harmful and that they just liked the sun they shared our home and garden with us. Then I looked out one day to see cows in the river down at the bottom of the garden and when I phoned Keith at work to tell him his workmates asked if I had a drinking problem? There would be frogs in the pool and thinking back on it when we bought the house the lady who owned it was sick in bed. Could this have been why? My husband was offered a transfer to Johannesburg. I wasn't looking forward to it as everyone told us how horrible it was but we found a place called Glenvista and it was so beautiful. Our house was built on the hills with great views and Karl's health improved greatly.

We were lucky to find a small house in amongst these huge expensive houses but what an outlook from the veranda. I hadn't been there long when I dreamt of my father putting branches into a vase and saying I am making an arrangement for you but the branches he was putting into the vase were black. I woke up knowing this was not good and thought my dad was going to die or me. Keith just laughed at me but I knew something was wrong. I checked my body and noticed a mark on my arm where I seemed to have scraped something. I was late in pregnancy with my third son Richard and when I was having a check-up with my gynaecologist I asked him to have a look at it. He told me it was just a broken blood vessel. I was relieved but something still niggled at me and when I was at my own doctor with my son who had a chest cold I asked him to have a look at it. The doctor took one look then immediately cut the mole out there and then and seemed very concerned. Further analysis revealed that it was a melanoma. I was quickly sent to a surgeon who cut out more of the surrounding area. He couldn't give me an anaesthetic because of my pregnancy so my arm was numbed but I was awake and he must have forgotten as I heard him say "Just about to drop a baby and she gets cancer". This dream had saved my life and I was lucky as the doctor told me if it was discovered six weeks later I could have lost my arm or worse as the type of cancer I had travels quickly. My beautiful baby Richard was delivered safely and all was well. I had survived to see my son and had many years to be with my children. I was also blessed to have two wonderful maids while I stayed in South Africa to look after my children called Betty and Veronica. Sadly Betty went out one weekend waving goodbye to us and then we got a phone call to say she had suffered a heart attack. We were all deeply saddened by her death, as she loved the children as her own. Then Veronica came to help us and she was a great cook and a medicine woman as I was about to find out. I have found that some people judge you because you had a maid but what they don't understand is that our maids were part of the family and we cared for them as they did for us. For many of them it was the only way they could make money in order to care for their family.

My remaining years in South Africa were happy and my holistic work was about to take off. I always had an interest in the tarot so went to classes, which guided me to being a healer to help others. I decided to learn Reiki, Indian head and shoulder massage and reflexology I loved these therapies. Around this time I had a beautiful little girl and named her Eleanor and my workmates thought it was hilarious that I called her by the same name. I told them it was an Irish thing.

Then the dreams started again, showing me working with Veronica and learning the ways of the shaman I started to take dizziness in real life and the doctors couldn't find the cause. I asked Veronica if she was a samgoma (medicine women) and she said yes she was. She offered to bring her father of the church to see me and he was the head Shaman. He came to my home and when he looked at me, he looked into my very soul. He said "You are covered in itchies." but this was something he couldn't have known as it was winter I was covered up, so yes he was right I was covered with itchies. He said my spirit guide was trying to connect to me and I must light candles and pray which I did.

He organised three other shaman to come to my house and they blessed me. They wanted to have a ceremony and kill a chicken to help my spirit rise quicker but I couldn't agree to that as I have always had a great love of all animals. We had a great ceremony with lots of food and through visions they said I must wear a cover for my head, which was half yellow and blue. They had this specially made with a sign of a cross in the centre like a nun would wear and told me to use this clothe when I carried out healings either by putting it on the client of wearing it on my head. I had to put out all the food that I loved for my ancestors and light lots of green candles for God, yellow for spirit and red for the ancestors. They prayed over me and put white beads on each wrist. A few weeks after this ceremony I meditated a lot on the candle each day and started to see golden patterns and they developed into golden mandalas it was so beautiful I could have sat all day in awe. These mandala patterns have got stronger through the years. I now lie at night in bed in awe watching these divine beings come in and work on me. This was an interesting time of my life and the Shaman offered to teach me about herbs. I turned this down due to not understanding the language as my maid Veronica translated for me. They wanted me to attend their church at the time, which I would have loved to do but it was quite dangerous for a white woman to go to the townships. They give me a cloth of the lion as in my dreams I walked with the lions.

CHAPTER 3

Coming Home

I loved Africa but knew it was time to return home, Keith got an offer of a transfer to Scotland for 4 years and we took it and we are still here 14 years later.

My path led me back to Scotland and it was difficult coming from the sun to severe weather and small houses again. I set up a healing room in my house and had another job in a nursery looking after babies. The golden mandala patterns were getting stronger and deities and angels were coming in through the centre while I carried out reiki treatments. We lived right by a forest and I knew this was great energy. My second son Paul came back from America where he had attended a golf academy for a few years and it was great to have my son back with me. The two younger children Richard and Elle settled in quite well but Richard had a problem with his nose and they discovered a tumour, thankfully it was not malignant but it was a challenge for the doctors to remove and an even bigger challenge for Richard to come through it but he did it, such a nightmare at such a young age, he went on to obtain his degree in animal biology and his masters in ecology, and is now doing his PHD.

Our eldest boy Karl was still in South Africa as he was still studying at university and we didn't want to disrupt him. He is now living in London and enjoying life and working in I.T.

Paul went on to university and become an engineer and is now living in Brisbane, Australia with his beautiful Irish wife Roisin and their darling baby Jack. They are having a great adventure. Elle is studying Graphic Design and she hasn't had a easy life but she has turned out stronger through it all but still yearns for Africa as she had such great memories there.

We had a few good years until disaster struck again. Would I be so lucky the second time around?

CHAPTER 4

The Diagnosis

I had just been to my nephew's wedding and the next day we had a barbeque at my sister and brother in law's and we decided to have a group reiki session. My niece Claire noticed a lump on my foot and at the time I decided to ignore it. One year later it come into my head again and I thought I would try and pin point where the problem was on my body. This led me to my adrenal gland and my sternum. Around my sternum felt a little weird. Was it a lump? So off I went to the doctor who thought everything was ok and nothing to worry about but she asked if I would be happier checking it out and I said yes. Then the call come from the doctor saying they found something in my right lung and I would need to go for a further scan. The radiologist asked if I had pain or sickness and I said no. All the time I was thinking I am ok. I kept it from my children until I was told for sure what it was. My daughter sensed something was wrong and remembered seeing a letter I got through to go to hospital and asked me about this. I told her what was happening and Elle went to the doctor with me. It was a great support to have her there I felt a great comfort and strength from her when the doctor told me I had a mass a size of a golf ball in my right lung. I would have to go for a biopsy and am glad no one warned me about that, as it wasn't the nicest experience. I was still hoping it was an abscess or some other growth. Richard and Elle were a great strength to me and pretended to be coping with all this as I was too. I went to see the doctor the following week who informed me it was cancer, a very rare cancer. They talked about surgery but it was in an awkward spot so first of all they wanted to see if it had spread and sent me for a PET scan. My son Rich came with me and I was so glad that we were both strong and keeping each other up. We were both thinking an operation would get rid of this forever and although it would be a big operation I was OK with that. The doctor called me from the waiting room and I was trying to read his face. He was smiling and seemed very pleasant but what a shock to us both when he said it had spread to my adrenal gland and it was inoperable. He spoke something about chemo and a tablet but I didn't hear much after that as I just saw Richard's face and knew he was sinking faster than me. How we both got home that day I don't remember. I spent a lot of time in bed trying to come to terms with this. I hadn't had anything I couldn't cope with before and it was hard to understand what was happening to me. I wanted to waken and find it was just a nightmare but it wasn't – it was happening. I hadn't ever smoked how could this be happening? My visions started in my dreams, one I had with red crosses on my white slippers and white shirts with red crosses on them. Then I saw little capsules with red crosses on them. Could this be my cells being protected? I also had visions of all the war graves with white crosses with red poppies on them was I going through this to help the people who died in the war. Was this a release of suffering for these brave people? It was around Ascension time in December 2012 when all this happened a very special time for spiritual people and the world was moving into a higher vibration, which I was hoping was in my favour. I had yet another dream that Doreen, my sister-in-law would go through ascension too and I would go through it in a completely different way which I certainly did.

Doreen has always been there for me sending reiki distant healing during my journey and giving me reiki treatments, which I was very grateful for. She has been a great support, as was my friend Amy whose messages from the angels and reiki healings have given me such strength and comfort. I am blessed to have two wonderful souls to help me through this and I love you both.

Richard would have to get out of the house and stay overnight to release his sadness and return pretending to be coping and I knew he was falling apart. Elle had to be strong and hold it together as she had nowhere to go to release the sadness and I had to try and make it easy for them. Karl was in London so was away from it and I hoped this eased things for him but he always tried to keep my spirits up with humour telling me he would get me a purple wig but underneath he was struggling. Karl has a gift of making us laugh. Keith my husband doesn't show his emotions very well but he was shocked and tried to understand it all too. I had to break the news to my son Paul and daughter-in-law Roisin in Australia, which I was dreading. I decided to Skype (wrong decision) and Richard said he would sit with me and help me and that comforted me a lot. I will never forget the look on Paul's face. I should have phoned as he was struggling. My son who is the protector of the family and looks after us couldn't take this away for me and he couldn't erase it. Roisin was also devastated and was trying to understand it all. I couldn't protect them from this news and to feel their pain caused me great heartache.

I had an appointment with a consultant a few weeks later but inside I was numb. I couldn't show it or cry, I had to keep strong for my family. No one can describe what you are going through but my children and husband encouraged me to talk about it, which was a great help.

Chapter 5

A Spark of Hope

$\mathcal{I}$ remember doing my tarot cards the day before my appointment with the consultant and the Archangel Michael came up with the healing and miracle card. Excited I showed my children and they tried for my sake to look happy. We all went as a family to the consultant's room and by this time I wasn't feeling. I was just in trance mode. Dr Nicolson, a very strong vibrant woman understood how I felt, angry and alone. I had never smoked in my lifetime and never had any chest trouble. She told me she could give me a tablet, which was very effective for this type of cancer and could prolong my life for years. I was a genetic match for this tablet and I thanked God for that. I felt a spark of hope come back to me and my eyes filled up. I had some time I could hold on too and I knew this was a window of opportunity to work through my cancer and to help others and myself. Dr Nicholson had opened the door of life for me and for that I am so very grateful.

The family were so happy and Doctor Nicholson got a huge hug from me. Things were so different going back to the car, everyone was joyous. I phoned my sons in London and Australia with the good news and we all danced with joy. I knew then that God had a plan for me and my spark of hope grew from that day. I realised I had all my healing experience to tap into what was I thinking. I started the tablet over Christmas time and it was great at first. Then

I got these rashes and felt very itchy but I had to be very careful when using sprays and creams and after an antibiotic it settled down. Then I started to experience dizziness and sickness but I wondered if this could be the same as my first experience of dizziness in South Africa when the shaman told me a spirit guide was trying to connect with me. My daughter Elle has been my angel through my journey and has always been there for me and she would get me into bed where I would fall into a deep sleep and have lots of visions. Richard was also a great support, he then got a job as a ranger and went to the Isle of Arran over the summer so it was good for him to get away for a while.

I have the most extraordinary children all with such different personalities and career paths and yet so intuitive, close and happy with such a strong heart connection and all of them share a great sense of humour. I love my children with all my heart and am so proud of them – and my husband Keith and my beautiful daughter-in-laws Roisin and Wendy and my darling angel grandson Jack. I am blessed to have them all in my life!

CHAPTER 6

The Shaman

T went on a trip to Ireland where Doreen had arranged a visit to a Shaman. His name was Paul, a friendly man with a strong Irish accent. He told me my mum was lost in the dimensions and wasn't with my dad and proceeded to reunite my mother and dad in spirit. Mum was lost and too afraid to move from where she was. I felt so good after that and felt my visit had been worthwhile. My mum died from lung cancer and because she was suffering in another dimension it could have potentially been affecting me on earth but now she was at peace and back with dad.

When I returned after a month or so I had a strong urge to see another shaman and found Jason in Scotland who was amazing. He lived in a little cottage way in the hills and he talked a lot to me at first. Then he put me on a treatment bed and I held two large crystals. My body shook the whole time he treated me as he played the drum and I loved that he told me I was completely surrounded in huge slabs of crystal and that he hadn't ever seen anything like this before. He said "I don't know what the higher powers have in store for you" but he was told to put crystal tetrahedrons around my pelvic area. I do a meditation called the Merkaba, which places you in a tetrahedron, a sacred geometry shape and I was amazed at that. A nun also came through and said she was Sister Clara of the order of the white swan and said they helped the soldiers in the war. She told me that I must breathe deeply and relax to find my true self. He also told me I had something on the right just below my waist and later I found out I had a very small tumour on the right side of my bowel, which I had from the beginning. Thankfully, it has now been removed. Jason had to use a swan feather to close off the treatment as the higher beings had requested this and so he had to go looking for one in his bundle of feathers. He said he had never been asked to do this before and then he was told to give me the feather, I had brought him a gift of oil so I didn't feel so bad. Jason had made me aware of many things and I am grateful for his help.

I began to do research into nuns and the order of the white swan and up came the druids and the bards and Saint Brigit, who was the first nun. I discovered that she was also known as the white swan. She was a nun, a healer who loved animals and helped the poor people. She was the patron Saint of Ireland alongside Saint Patrick. Saint Brigit apparently delivered Jesus and is the goddess of midwifes. Could I have found a past lifetime? I could relate to all these things in my life as I absolutely love children, animals and healing. The weird thing is apparently Saint Brigit's head lies in a chapel in Lisbon. Is that why I have had migraines from such a young age and why I can see the most beautiful golden mandalas? Apparently Saint Brigit was interested in alchemy and had a book of the most beautiful patterns that were apparently not man-made but miraculous. Saint Brigit is buried with St Patrick not far from were I used to live in Ireland and I have been to the grave when I was quite young. I remember waking up in South Africa feeling my heart beating strongly through another body it was a body lying on a stone slab in a cave but it had no head that was quite frightening for me.

I believe we have lived many lifetimes and if you can connect to the higher version of you then you have found your true power.

The last Shaman I went to was in Ireland called Anne who had a gift of being in your visions with you and she brought me into a visualisation. Anne remarked someone had come to meet me and asked me who it was I said "God" but she corrected me that it was Jesus I was in awe. I felt a great bonding connection and I cried and cried. I was so emotional and Anne was nearly crying too. She said I had to connect to Jesus again and she wasn't to know the reason why. Anne said if I ever need to speak to him I can connect to him and he will be there if I have any problems or need to talk. That just blew me away and I was walking on air after that.

It is up to you if you want to visit a shaman but you can see how they all helped me in different ways.

Amy had contacted me about a vivid dream she had and in the dream while working on me she said she could see into my heart were there was a baby, I was teaching him and he was opening my heart. I asked Amy during an angel reading if it could have been my grandson Jack and she said yes it was. So I also have my grandson to thank for opening my heart chakra before he was even born. Thank you my darling Jack.

What a mysterious and wonderful world we live in.

CHAPTER 7

Healing ways

Reason

*T*he shamans believe where your cancer is can be an indication of what is going on deeper inside you. Our doctors will treat the symptoms but you can look deeper into the cause.

Lung	- grief
Liver	- anger
Stomach	- worry
Kidney	-fear

Look inside yourself

Sometimes when cancer comes it can be a sign for you to look deeper into your life situation. Is your heart so closed due to emotional upset that you have been pushing issues to the back of you heart and not dealing with them? Look deeper into yourself. Are you happy? Arc you able to speak your truth or do you often not want to express yourself so you bottle it up? These things could be causing sickness for you. Express yourself with love. Be your own person and change these things if need be. Do not blame others and keep your heart warm and the people who love you close by. I couldn't have done this without my loving family. My cancer was in the lung. I wasn't living to my full potential and my heart had closed. This was a kick in the backside for me. I am here for a purpose but I did not realise how big that purpose was.

On my journey I have tried many different methods and I hope they help to motivate you. There is no particular order. Just do anything you are drawn to, that you feel you would enjoy, and blend them into your everyday life.

You will go through darkness, hopelessness and loneliness at first but you will come through the other side stronger and more determined.

I know it's difficult to come to terms with the challenges that lie ahead and you need to take the time to go inside yourself to question things and understand until you are ready to ignite the spark, move on and heal.

Are you living someone else's dreams?
Are you being your true self?
Are you living in fear?
In your heart do you feel love joy and smile?

Connect to Mother Earth and Father Sky

My sons Paul and Karl paid for my fare to Australia and when I went there Paul and Roisin took us to a remote island out in the wilds. I bathed in a blue lagoon every evening and got into the water and put my head under and baptised myself whenever I could. The lagoon was surrounded with trees native to Australia and they released tea tree oil into the lagoon. The water felt lovely and it made my skin so soft and healed the sores on my head from the tablet.

Also bathing in the salt of the seawater I connected to mother earth and the beautiful sand and sat under the stars at night under Father Sky with a glass of wine. We watched the dolphins in amazement, slept in a tent that was a sacred geometry shape, the pyramid, and I felt blessed.

I am not saying everyone must go to Australia to heal but get to the nearest beach or beautiful place in nature and if you can get into the water, baptise yourself and connect to the earth and sky. Become the tree, let the roots go into the ground and the branches connect to the sky. I couldn't get insurance with terminal cancer and trying to speak to these people on the phone was very negative for me so I insured myself for everything else other than the cancer and went on to have a great adventure. Enjoy your life. It's your chance to start living and to connect to nature and release your fear. Find something that excites you!

Be one with spirit just be and live for each day always enjoy the present moment.

The Mind

The first thing that helped me was getting my mind right and this is the most important thing. You must be positive and do not let any negativity seep in. Feel that light come into your heart and you must believe you are well. Move away from the fear, shine your bright light into the cancer to reduce the power it has over you.

If you need to retreat do so or if you need to talk to someone tell them what you are thinking. You need to let go of fear so you can start living. Don't let cancer suffocate you but rather let it resuscitate you.

Surround yourself with happy people who laugh a lot

Negative people will drain you. Find calmness within yourself and believe. Move forward and don't look back.

What is it you love to do?

Do something each day that you love and enjoy. I loved walking in nature and feeding the birds, giving healings and spiritual work.

Dream yourself well

See yourself as radiant each day and energised and connected to the highest version of you. Invite your highest version of yourself into your heart. The world has a very high vibration now so tap into it. Be you, be free and dream.

Who should you tell?

I did tell my family circle but I decided not to tell my friends and neighbours about my illness. Sometimes people mean well but their negativity can drain your energy and you don't want to go into a downward spiral if they treat you differently. They don't know how to deal with this news and it makes things difficult for them too. You need to reduce the amount of time that you talk about being ill and refuse to allow illness a place in your consciousness.

Depending on your circumstances though if you are on your own you will need help and need the love of your friends and neighbours get comfort from them.

To work or not to work?

I continued working from my healing room as this is something I enjoyed so much. Remember do things you love to do. I lived as normal and I become grateful for every day and I was surrounded by love from all my family.

Reiki

I recommend Reiki treatments as they are so relaxing and allow you to go deeper and let go. It also opens up chakras, the energy wheels in your body, which may have closed and removes blockages in your body. If you are too tired because of chemo treatments you can get distance healing. A healer can send you healing energy and you don't have to leave your house. You can release a lot. I never realised I was holding on to so much stuff and I cried a lot during Reiki treatments and eventually my heart opened. Nurture yourself and arrange for some treatments, as your life is precious. The therapists kindly volunteer and treatments are free to cancer patients so enjoy them.

I also treated myself with Reiki, I am glad I had this knowledge to tap into. I also sent healing to myself and was shocked how strong this made me feel.

Pranic healing is also amazing. We are lucky to have such great healing modalities available to us these days. Take advantage of them.

Moving

Keep as active as you can
Move your body into unusual positions and stretch
Yoga or Qigong

Qigong

Qigong exercise ensures you have to keep moving and keep all your channels open. I have a very gentle exercise, which is great to get you going in the morning and moves the parts you wouldn't usually move. You have to keep the energy moving through you from heaven and earth.

I used the YouTube video "Deep breathing morning Qi gong – opening, cleansing and warming up by Bruno at Lotus Centre, Cambodia".

A simple remedy to lift your spirits

In many Shamanic societies if you come to a medicine man disheartened, dispirited or depressed, they would ask you 3 questions

"When did you stop dancing?"
"When did you stop singing?"
"When did you stop being enchanted by stories?"
Gabrielle Roth

Prayer

Don't underestimate the power of prayer. The shaman pray all the time something we don't do often enough. My mother every night would get down on her knees and pray.

Music

Dance to happy music. You will love this! It can be in your living room on your own or go to classes. Play old music or tunes that rekindles your youth and spirit. Start laughing, start enjoying and sing loudly!

Clothes

Wear bright clothes this simple act will brighten your spirit.

Meditation

Make sure you put aside some quiet time for yourself and meditate, slow your breath down and listen to the natural tide and rhythm of the breath. This is very grounding and relaxing. It calms the body so that you feel relaxed. Think of a happy occasion so it will help warm your heart and just bc in a bubble of love. Just be - relax and let go.

Guided Meditation on Youtube

"Inner Smile" by Qigong master Lee Holden
"Healing the Body, Mind & Spirit Meditation" uploaded by Kalawna Biggs

Higher Self

Connect to your higher self, the highest version of yourself. We all have a higher self, a more magnificent and radiant version of ourselves. Invite your higher self into your heart and join as one. When I close my eyes my higher self's eyes are always there looking into mine as if to say I am here and all is well. It is very comforting.

Thought

You are what you think so have wonderful images of yourself. Dream your life into being. See yourself radiant, surrounded with sparkles and bursting with happiness.

Diet

I changed my diet taking in more vegetables seeds and nuts. The green breakfast drinks are great with almond milk. Experiment and see what you enjoy. I do believe in the green vegetables. You can add all the greens and nuts you want and it still tastes so good. Introduce raw foods. Get great ideas on how to make vegetables appealing and the energy they give you is amazing. My breakfast is usually a green drink or organic corn flakes with grapes and yoghurt. In the evening I have pesto pasta with pine nuts, sun dried tomatoes, olives and spinach.

When you eat right you have great energy and you don't feel like sweet things, which is better for you at this time, and as I have a sweet tooth found it difficult but realised sweet stuff is a no no. I know how hard it is to give up sweet stuff but I have eventually woke up to this. You might fall off the wagon now and again but that's ok you will get back on track.

Ask the Angels

Don't bottle things up surrender and release to the angels. You must call in your archangels and angels. They are all around you but won't intervene until you ask them so bring in thousands of them and ask them to heal you. I have seen the angelic forces work on me every night. They can do so much for us. Archangel Raphael comes in often to work on my heart and Archangel Michael to cut all fear away and give me strength. Call on them before you fall asleep.

Affirmations are great...

The affirmation below is very beneficial given to us from Saint Germain and the legions of light.

"I am a being of violet fire I'm the purity god desires" say it in your mind while walking, saying it quicker as you go along – very powerful. If you are feeling tired and unable to walk, if getting chemo, say it in your mind at anytime. It envelops you in a violet light while the angels work on you. Instead of having negative thoughts while receiving chemo this is very uplifting.

Think positively, say the following affirmations before falling asleep at night and anytime during the day. Trust me. Just repeat

I am optimal Health

I am an abundance of health

I am an abundance of love

I am...... These are the two of the most powerful words and what you put after them shapes your reality. So use your words you need in your life at this moment.

Release Fear

This is about releasing all fear, starting to live and doing things you want to do.

It is about making each day a celebration. Release yourself from the fear of cancer and put it behind you. Don't feed the fear.

Push away those negative thoughts.

Sit in Nature

Connect to nature, sit in your garden and feel roots from your feet and branches from your head. Feel your heart open, feed the birds and enjoy watching them from inside your home or outside.

Tree Healing

Sit or stand by a tree and let the tree energy move through you. Don't worry what other people think. Who cares? Be yourself and ask the tree to take the sick energy. Hold your hands on the tree and your forehead touching open your heart to its energy.

Blessing your medicine

I blessed my tablet by putting the following Reiki signs into it:

The hon sha ze sho nen x 3
Sei he ki x 3
Cho ku rei x 3
Dai koo myo x 3

If you don't want to be attuned to Reiki that's ok you can use the sign of the cross x 3 and watch Mantak Chia "how to energise water and give it properties to cure disease" This great Master Mantak Chia has helped me with his videos and gives all his knowledge to others for free.

If you are receiving Chemo put the Reiki signs into the medicine or the sign of the cross these can be put in with your mind as I know its difficult when you sitting in a room with others while receiving chemo. See in your mind the signs go in or draw it on the medicine. Put the signs in x 3 and let your heart open. Think of a happy time and say to yourself "sick cells please listen this sacred medicine will take you to mother earth." Doing this you are asking the cancer to move into mother earth. I always felt good when saying this, isn't it amazing that you can talk to your cells.

Water

Drink plenty of water, I used Deeside Water known for its healing properties you can bless the water or blow on the water

Water blessings – blow on the water until it moves say "medicine of life" before drinking.

or

Say into the water "sick cells please listen this sacred water will take you to mother earth" which ever one appeals to you.

Every time you drink water talk to your cells.

Watch on YouTube "How to energise water" by Mantak Chia as he shows you how exactly to do it and shows you each step. How to hold it to your heart feeling of love and feeling grateful and connecting to the mind and saying "This sacred water will give me health, wealth and longevity". You will feel so good after this.

More Mantak Chia YouTube videos to look at and do your own research

"Healing practice (The breath of Life)"

"Inner Smile for daily Life."

"Micro Cosmic Orbit"

6 Healing sounds
Lung – sssssss
Kidney – Chooo
Liver Sound - Shhhhh
Heart Sound - hawwwww
Spleen and pancreas - Whooooo
Triple warmer - heeeeee

Angel Cards

I choose 3 angel cards each morning. Getting messages is very uplifting. Buy yourself a box, whichever ones you are drawn too.

Angel Messages

The messages from the angels supported me and comforted me through my journey. Treat yourself to a reading.

Calling in the 4 Archangels

Go into your favourite room light some candles and incense sticks and you can put on some relaxing music if you would like. Use a compass to find out the 4 directions in your room. Define a circle in the room by walking clockwise x 3 times around in a circle before entering this gives you a magic circle. You can have a chair in the middle of the circle for you to sit after evoking the Archangels.

Remember you can use your own words when calling in the Archangels. Whatever you feel comfortable with. Feel the connection in your heart.

Extend your arms and face east and say "Archangel Raphael Great Guardian of the east please protect and guide me during this healing. I am so grateful for your presence today and all the healing you do for me".

Keep your arms extended and turn to the south this time address Michael

"Archangel Michael great guardian of the South please protect a guide me through this healing. I want you to know that I am grateful to you for giving me courage, strength and the ability to speak the truth".

Still your arms outstretched, face the west and speak to Gabriel.

"Archangel Gabriel Great Guardian of the West please protect and guide me throughout this healing. I am grateful to you for all your guidance, inspiration and purification."

Turn now to the North and speak to Uriel

"Archangel Uriel great guardian of the north please protect me though out this healing. I am grateful to you for providing me with tranquillity, peace of mind and the ability to give and receive".

Sit or kneel or lie in the centre of your circle and visualise yourself surrounded by the love and protection of the 4 archangels. You can just sit and meditate or pray in this sacred space and feel them work on you feel them around your body and in your hair. Be ready to receive some messages. You can communicate with these beautiful and powerful angels. When finished go around each direction with arms outstretched and thank them individually starting with Archangel Uriel in the north and Archangel Gabrielle in the west, Archangel Michael in the south and Archangel Raphael in the east. You can use this sacred space when receiving chemo if you are in a room of your own but only if you feel comfortable with this or in your own home you can prepare your space before the nurse arrives.

Candles

You can light candles at anytime around your home.

Light candles and pray
Green for God
Yellow for spirit
Red for ancestors

Salt Baths

I use Himalayan pink crystal salts as it clears your aura (an energy field around your body) you can also use Epsom salts, which needs no soaking. Put the Himalayan salts in some mineral water to dissolve the crystals the night before and add this to your bath. It is very good for your skin and you can soak up all those minerals in the salts. Add some lavender oil if you like.

After your bath use oils

Use Solum Comp oil and rub it onto your skin. This is a peat oil so you are connecting to the earth and the magical peat people. Rub it all over and enjoy the beautiful aroma – use on your solar plexus if you need calmed.

In your heart feel the love and joy and smile

Breathing

Most of us breathe too shallow and quickly in our day to day lives. Some people barely breathe at all. It is essential we learn to breathe deeper during the day. When you want to meditate or just relax breathe in deeply until you feel your belly rise hold for 7 and let go pushing the breath deep into the belly for 8, letting your shoulders relax, it will allow oxygen to go to the brain and help your cells as well as release tension in your body.

Release stress

Breathe in deeply and let it go in a sigh. Do this when you feel tense.

Sound Healing

Doreen's friend Sandra kindly gave me a free sound healing when I was in Ireland. It was so good and I felt the sound work on my chakras and envelop me. Experience a sound healing you will love it

There is also a sound healing on YouTube "The Tibetan bells", which I found very effective. I listened to one for healing trees but the frequency might not agree with everyone but I enjoyed it and it starts with a beautiful Gayatri Mantra the Buddha would come in while I meditated. It is called "Tibetan healing bowl – Deep esoteric healing vibrations" by Atommachine. If that one doesn't work for you the other I would recommend, and I felt the angels come in immediately, meditate to Jonathan Goldman – "Holy harmony (healing frequencies)".

The rain stick is very grounding put it on your solar plexus and turn it around. It is also good to ground children.

The Zaphir wind chimes they come in different tunings and are another healing instrument and very relaxing you can buy them online and listen to the soft chimes. They have a magical sound and effect.

Sacred Geometry

The sacred geometry shapes are very beneficial for you. Imagine you lying under a bright coloured pyramid shape and feeling safe and secure when you go to bed at night or while receiving chemo.

Dreams

Analyse your dreams, write them down and think about them. What messages are they sending you?

Another dream I had which led me to hand reflexology. I was inside my body and looking through a porthole window at high wild water and I didn't feel good. Then I moved into a room, up a little bit and suddenly I was calm. After analysing this I knew I had moved into my solar plexus, which is a part of your body that makes you feel calm.

Reflexology

I used hand reflexology to massage my solar plexus and to keep myself calm during my dizzy spells. Get yourself a diagram of the points on your hand, which you can find online, to see where you need to massage. I do foot reflexology but it can be awkward working on your own feet. You will be amazed when you see the different areas on your hand and massaging them can be very helpful or treat yourself to a foot reflexology session.

Crystals

Pick a crystal that you are attracted to and sit and hold it while meditating or have one around your neck. See which one speaks to you.

Colour

Meditate and whatever colour comes in let it flood your body as that is the colour you need to soak in.

Flower of Life

I do the Merkaba meditation and if you are drawn to being closer to your higher self and meditating in a tetrahedron sacred geometry shape I recommend going to a workshop.

Lastly, I had a great dream that the cancer would leave me as a tarantula walking away from me and I would just watch it go. I remember thinking in the dream should I catch it in a spider catcher and put it outside but I am glad I didn't. Just let it go!

Munay Ki Rites

I knew my trip to Ireland was an important trip as I was to receive the Munay ki Rites, the sacred rites handed down to the Inka people from the Archangels. To receive these rites from my sister in law Doreen was a blessing for me. I am forever grateful to Doreen for giving me these rites.

Usually one must spend many years in sacred study before receiving these rites but now they can be passed from human to human. The Elders believe that we are at a critical time in human history and the rites need to be transmitted to as many people as possible. I know passing these rites is both our destinies and it is a blessing and a joy for us to do this. I am grateful for Alberto Villoldo and the Shaman of Peru for bringing these rites to us in the west.

Through the 10 Sacred Munay Ki Rites

The Chakras are cleared

Protection is provided from the negative energies on earth.

A greater connection is made to the luminous beings.

A greater connection is made to the archetype beings and animal of the light that are linked to the shamanic traditions and each chakra.

Wisdom and divine power open up.

Genetic and karmic patterns that do not serve the highest good are released and healed.

The rites anchor each of the critical junctures in the process of becoming Homo Luminous as we transit from the body of humans to a transcended light being.

A few thoughts

It is remarkable to hear comments from the doctors "You don't reflect your medical records"

and

"If I didn't know you were sick, I couldn't tell from your chest x-ray as it looks normal"

After being stopped a few times on my travels by airport staff asking "is this you in the passport" so I asked them "Do I look better or worse" they answered "Much better" so I walk off smiling to myself.

I believe the last layer of cancer will be lifted as my dream has told me and was confirmed by an angel reading from Amy.

Believe in yourself and keep positive, feel it in your body. The main thing is to keep your inner light glowing that is the secret.

Through this journey I have found myself and my destiny as a healer and been guided to give the Munay Ki rites see where your journey will lead you.

I don't think of the cancer anymore I am too busy enjoying and embracing life and I am off to Australia for three months, thanks to Paul and Roisin, for my first cuddle of my little grandson Jack. Isn't life good?

I hope to have a healing centre some day where Doreen and I can reach out to people who need Reiki Attunements, Reiki treatments, Reflexology, Indian Head and Shoulder Massage, someone to talk to, meditations and a sanctuary they can go to to feel safe and loved and most importantly to receive the sacred Munay Ki Rites.

If you choose to like us on Facebook we are "The Munay Ki sisters."

I am moving back to Northern Ireland to a little place called Donaghadee as the motherland is calling me, its time to go home to that magical place and such beautiful people who make me smile.

Much love and blessings to each and every one of you as you embark on your journey and enjoy making it your own extraordinary and magical experience.

I am still on my spiritual journey and will continue to be a warrior of light to help others, thank you for walking with me.

Love and lots of angels Eleanor

A Note from My Children

" $\mathcal{M}$ y mom is my very best friend I can literally talk to her about anything, which I have friends I can do this with too, but it is different. My mom knows me inside out, she knows how I think, she always understands how I feel, even when I am being unreasonable my mom knows exactly how to make me feel on top of the world again. She has stuck by me in times when if I look back I couldn't have judged her for not standing by me. She is irreplaceable as a mother and my best friend. That's why when this happened to her it almost broke me the idea of loosing my very best friend tore me apart. It was difficult for all of us and I have been there for my mom as much as I possibly could but through all of this she has lived up to what she has always been, an amazing woman. Her positive attitude and her beliefs amaze me because they have not only helped her get through it but me too more than she will ever know. My mom's been through so much but still has a smile on her face and laughs everyday. I still have my best friend and I know I will for a long time."

Elle

"There are times in life when we all face challenges and throughout all the difficult times I have faced in my life there is always one person I can rely on, my mother. I have learnt right and wrong from my parents and have always

45

relied on their wisdom and experience when I feel like I'm out of my depth. My mom has always been a dedicated and loving parent as well as being my most thoughtful and supportive friend. She has helped to shape the person I am today and has given me every opportunity in life to discover who I am and where I want to go. Without her help and guidance my life would not have been the wonderful journey that it has been so far. As for what lies ahead, I have watched as my mom overcame this tragic set of circumstances with such grace, dignity and resilience. Her incredible courage and determination in the face of overwhelming adversity will always be an inspiration to me."

Richard

"If you had the option to go back in time to change things would you? If you think it would make your life easier and all your worries go away, would this be the case? Life is full of challenges and to face fear, endure grief, overcome worry, and strive for happiness is all part of a successful journey. My journey has been full of success, but not without its challenges.

I thank my parents for guiding me and placing me on this wonderful adventure. Mom, you play a big role in my success story and reading yours has been difficult but inspiring. Keep enjoying life and never look back. "Love you."

Paul

Title: MY HERO

PAST

My Mom and Dad left Northern Ireland to settle in South Africa in 1982 and I was 2 years old. We lived in Pinetown, South Africa just outside Durban City. Our house was on the perimeter of a game reserve so as a child it was very exciting. We often had snakes in our garden, deer passing running past the property fencing, the odd swarm of bees to escape from by locking ourselves in the house and legavaans (big lizards) swimming in our pool or toasting themselves on the brick face of the house wall. We even had a pet chameleon. It seemed normal at the time but when I look back I realise I could not have wished for a better place to grow up than South Africa ... we were very lucky to have such an abundance of wilderness and excitement on our doorstep.

Unfortunately Durban did come with drawbacks as it was really humid and the perfect breeding ground for germs and I spend a lot of my early childhood very sick. The worst being meningitis and viral pneumonia on multiple occasions. I can't remember how many times I was stuck in bed recovering from another illness ... I was tired of being sick but my Mom was always at my side. When I had a temperature she would have a damp cloth on my head day or night. When I was feeling low she was stroking my head putting me at peace. When I was in the hospital on my birthday she cheered me up with a helicopter cake. He-man was no match for my Supermom.

PRESENT

I arrived in London in 2003 ready for an adventure. My parents had moved to Aberdeenshire from South Africa in 2000. I was going to fly up to surprise them as soon as I'd worked up some cash in London. South African rands didn't convert to much in London so I started work as a painter decorator. It was honest work and labour paid really well in the UK and 3 weeks later I arrived outside the front door of my parents home. I couldn't wait to see the expression on my moms face and she didn't disappoint. Happiness expressed with a combination of screams and tears.

With my family's support I found an IT position in Stirling, Scotland a couple months later. The brilliance of the Scottish architecture amazed me. I was living in the town of Scottish heroes: The William Wallace monument stood proud on a hill above the University and Andrew Murray was already making waves in the tennis world. All this coupled with the mystery of a new start and meeting new people was incredible.

On the contrary my first couple months were difficult, I realised very quickly the social groups in Stirling included: students, footballers and pensioners. There was no group for South Africans in their mid-twenties. It was my time in life to grow up and learn to integrate into a new cultures and it was a lot tougher than I ever expected. I started getting bad chest pains attributed to anxiety and stress. I had never experienced anything like this before but my Mom was always a phone call away and she always put everything into perspective. If I am ever feeling stressed or overwhelmed with life I just give my Mom a call and my worries disappear.

Daenerys Stormborn is no match for the queen of my dragons.

REALITY

The phone rings and its my Mom on the line and as soon as I hear her voice I sense this isn't good news and I immediately prepare myself to be strong. My mom has Cancer ... I bite my tongue and immediately start talking about her road to recovery because I don't want to consider the reality in my face. My nervous reaction is to try and make people laugh so I start joking with my Mom that she will finally be able to try a variety of hairstyles if she goes down the chemotherapy route ... I know it's poor but it's not a comedy subject and I am doing my best.

Who will sit at my Moms bedside when she needs help, who will she call when she needs encouragement and support. What I forget is my mom is the strongest person I know, she isn't scared of cancer, the only fear she has is not being around to pick her children up when they fall. She has always been our pillar of strength.

My mother has been fighting cancer for 3 years. The cancer is now in remission because ....., Cancer is no match for my Mother ... My HERO

Karl

ACKNOWLEDGEMENTS

To Dr Nicholson and her wonderful team. Thank you for opening the door to life for me. Also for helping me on my journey and to all the researchers, whom I have never met, thank you.

To Dr O'Kelly and his team, thank you for making it possible for more trips to Australia. Thank you for working your magic yet again.

To my husband Keith, and my children, Elle and Richard, Paul and Roisin and little baby Jack and Karl and Wendy. Thank you to you all for your support and generosity and for surrounding me with love and nurturing me during my journey. I have the most wonderful family I am so blessed and grateful. I couldn't have done it without you all.

My sister-in-law Doreen for sending me distance Reiki from the very beginning for being there for me and supporting me through out this journey. To Doreen and John for their kindness the laughter and my retreats in Ireland and the Lake District and all the Reiki treatments and the most important Munay Ki rites. My soul sister we came through it together I am deeply thankful.

To my friend Amy for all the Reiki treatments, get-togethers and wonderful memories, messages and guidance from the angels who have supported and comforted me throughout the journey. I truly am blessed to have such a good friend.

To my sister Gwen for her generosity, hospitality, kindness and who has been there for me throughout my journey and when I needed a shoulder to lean on you supported me with love. Thank you.

To my sister in law Valerie and husband Errol for all their support given to me, and for their great hospitality, laughter and kindness and all the fun and laughter and memories we have had both in Ireland and Scotland.

To my brother Derick and wife Carole for their kindness, hospitality and support. To their son, my nephew, Dr Stephen Tate for all his help and support given to me when I got diagnosed and throughout my journey.

To my brother Roy and wife Vivienne for their kindness, hospitality and support. Even though they are in Australia we are always close in heart.

To all my family circle nephews, nieces and cousins both here and abroad for all your kind thoughts and to you Lily for your daily prayers thank you.

To the Shaman on my journey Paul, Jason and Anne. Thank you for providing me with a look into the different dimensions and making me realise I have always been between the world of the Shaman and the Angels.

To Master Mantak Chia thank you for making your videos and all you teachings free to the world. We are blessed.

To Alberto Villoldo and the Shaman for bringing the Munay Ki Rites back to the western world and for teaching us ways to live an extraordinary life in full health.

To my angels, masters, teachers and loved ones and every one of my spiritual beings from the light who have always supported me thank you.

Printed in the United States
By Bookmasters